TRUTH IN THE TEACHING OF MASTER NUNO OLIVEIRA

Eleanor Russell

The Truth in the Teaching of Nuno Oliveira

First Published in Australia, 2001. Reprinted 2005 & 2010.

Copyright © 2001, E&E Russell

ISBN: 0646498509

This edition: *Truth in the Teaching of Master Nuno Oliveira*

Copyright © 2015, Xenophon Press

Photography by Eleanor Russell

All rights reserved. No part of this work may be reproduced or transmitted in any form or by any means, electronic or mechanical, including photocopying, or by any information storage or retrieval system except by written permission from the publisher.

Published by Xenophon Press LLC
7518 Bayside Road, Franktown, Virginia 23354-2106, USA
XenophonPress@gmail.com
1/757.414.0393

www.XenophonPress.com

Xenophon Press Edition ISBN: 9780933316768

French Edition: *Notes d'Eleanor Russell sur l'enseignement de Nuno Oliveira*

ISBN: 9782701191812

XENOPHON PRESS LIBRARY

Xenophon Press is dedicated to the preservation of classical equestrian literature. We bring both new and old works to English-speaking riders. Available at www.XenophonPress.com

30 Years with Master Nuno Oliveira, Henriquet 2011
A New Method to Dress Horses, Cavendish 2015
A Rider's Survival from Tyranny, de Kunffy 2012
Another Horsemanship, Racinet 1994
Art of the Lusitano, Yglesias de Oliveira 2012
Austrian Art of Riding, Poscharnigg 2015
Breaking and Riding, Fillis 2015
Baucher and His School, Decarpentry 2011
Dressage in the French Tradition, Diogo de Bragança 2011
The Art of Riding a Horse, or, Description of Modern Manège, D'Eisenberg 2015
École de Cavalerie Part II, Robichon de la Guérinière 1992, 2015
Equine Osteopathy: What the Horses Have Told Me, Ginaux 2014
François Baucher: The Man and His Method, Baucher/Nelson 2013
Great Horsewomen of the 19th Century in the Circus, Nelson 2015
Gymnastic Exercises for Horses Volume II, Russell 2013
H. Dv. 12 Cavalry Manual of Horsemanship, Reinhold 2014
Handbook of Jumping Essentials, Lemaire de Ruffieu 1997
Handbook of Riding Essentials, Lemaire de Ruffieu 2015
Healing Hands, Giniaux, VMD 1998
Horse Training: Outdoors and High School, Beudant 2014
Legacy of Master Nuno Oliveira, Millham 2013
Methodical Dressage of the Riding Horse, Faverot de Kerbrech 2010
Racinet Explains Baucher, Racinet 1997
Science and Art of Riding in Lightness, Stodulka 2015
The Art of Traditional Dressage, Volume I DVD, de Kunffy 2013
The Ethics and Passions of Dressage Expanded Ed., de Kunffy 2013
The Gymnasium of the Horse, Steinbrecht 2011
The Italian Tradition of Equestrian Art, Tomassini 2014
The Maneige Royal, de Pluvinel 2010, 2015
The Portuguese School of Equestrian Art, de Oliveira/da Costa 2012
The Spanish Riding School & Piaffe and Passage, Decarpentry 2013
To Amaze the People with Pleasure and Delight, Walker 2015
Total Horsemanship, Racinet 1999
Truth in the Teaching of Master Nuno Oliveira, Russell 2015
Wisdom of Master Nuno Oliveira, de Coux 2012

TRUTH IN THE TEACHING OF MASTER NUNO OLIVEIRA

CONTENTS	PAGE
Introduction	9
General Comments	11
The Rider	14
The Aids — Back, Seat, and Weight	17
The Aids — The Rider's Legs	21
The Aids — Spurs / Rider's Hands	24
Horses' Movement	30
Work with the Lunge	38
Young Horses	43
Relaxation of the Horse	44
Halt and Rein Back	47
Circles	50
Circles/Serpentines	52
Beginning Shoulder-In	55
Shoulder-In	56
Half-Pass	62
Eye, Mouth & Jaw	71
Cadence — Impulsion	77
Lightness — Collection	81
The Centre Line	83
Pirouettes	85
Piaffe	91
Passage	95
Pillars	97
Spanish Walk	99
End of Class	103

And, always, afterwards...a caress with love.

INTRODUCTION

NUNO OLIVEIRA…For most of the equestrian world the name says it all!

Born in Portugal on 25th June 1925, Nuno Oliveira began learning his chosen profession at an early age with his Master, Joaquin Gonzales de Miranda.

Nuno Oliveira learned the principles of de la Guérinière and Marialva, and he never deviated from these Classical Principles in training horses throughout his life.

He retained Mr Miranda's beliefs in great discipline and calmness from both horse and rider – as well as the continued study of the writings of the Old Masters.

I was fortunate enough to spend almost 12 months in Nuno Oliveira's village of Avessada, Portugal, riding my French stallion, Victorieux.

It was during that time I was given permission to take these photographs… some of which appear in this book.

A short time prior to Nuno Oliveira's death in February, 1989, he and I were looking at the projected book and the use of the photos.

The text is simply quotes of Nuno Oliveira and from my notes over 10 years. He was most enthusiastic about the project. I remember mentioning to him at the time, that in some photos he did not look perhaps as perfect we all wish we did in photos.

He thought for a minute and then said, "But the serious rider will look beyond that."

Towards the end of his life he was frequently in pain, but he continued riding his beloved horses.

As a trainer he shared his knowledge with his students with a generosity I will never forget – always with endless patience he would discuss a horse's problem and the suggested solution.

His students will especially remember at day's end the glass of vino in his office and the detailed discussions of some of the movements and achievements of the horses and riders that day.

I hope the publishing of these photographs and words is a help, however small, to his many students around the world who miss Nuno Oliveira.

— Eleanor Russell

• The horses in the photos are: *Soante* (the brown horse); *Bunker* (the bigger chestnut horse); and *Balet* (young, chestnut three-year-old horse).

GENERAL COMMENTS

"The choice of horse must first be a love affair."

AMONG the daily cares and concerns of life, each rider can, while thinking of the moments of beauty he has spent with his horse or horses, be sure that riding is an art.

One man in general is the same as another, but it is quite different if he lives in another climate and country. So it is the same for the horse.

Nuno Oliveira often quoted General L'Hotte...

"Horses always remember their first habits."

When I choose a horse I look first to see if I like its general appearance, its beauty and the expression in its eyes.

I look at him through half closed eyes as he is led, in hand towards me to see if his general appearance is well rounded, even if he is not well nourished. Finally I look more closely at all of his gaits then I look at his legs.

A good horse is no particular colour nor a particular breed. There are good horses and bad horses in every breed but some breeds have a greater number of horses suited for one thing or another.

Observe the state of mind of the horse while it moves without being excited or pushed. I watch how the back functions in all gaits. The back is the bridge between the fore and hind legs and the part that carries the rider's weight.

A horse is an animal who has more rapid reflexes than a man and has enormous sensitivity. The horse is astonishingly quick to understand his rider's mood and to feel and hear all influences.

When the rider feels and loves his horse, working to help his horse develop both physically and mentally, it is now that a rapport will develop that the horse will never forget. If the horse and rider are perhaps separated for

The choice of horse must first be a love affair.

some years, when reunited the horse will remember his rider's aids and the rapport will again be there.

If the trainer forgets that the memory of a horse is truly amazing then the trainer will be confronted with many difficulties during dressage training. This amazing memory of the horse remains of great importance throughout his entire training.

Your voice, caresses, and other rewards will stay in his mind as will violent blows or other severe methods of punishment which will cause loss of confidence and nervousness.

Ask for much, be content with little and reward often.

Horses who have a bad character are rare. In general their problems are caused by insensitive, thoughtless, inexperienced or unkind riders. Explaining to the horse always with gentle ways will give him confidence and show him there is nothing to fear. But he must understand and accept without resistance whatever you ask him to do. You must reward the horse each time he does what you ask of him, but never ask more than he is capable of giving. This will make him your friend and not your slave.

Every horse is a person, with a nervous system different.

Nuno Oliveira quoted Steinbrecht: "That for correct work the conformation of the horse's back is of decisive importance, and, that during the horse's training it must be the centre of attention."

Correct dressage training can change a horse. It can give him a different balance and outline as his muscles develop. This improvement can sometimes cause considerable surprise!

I have often had to work with two different types of horse, and I have observed that one system of training cannot always be exactly the same for both horses. Each one must, of course, be worked according to Classical Principles but you must feel sometimes the differences in the horses and allow for it.

THE RIDER

FIRST a relaxed mind then a relaxed horse.

A relaxed horse is a calm horse…He is not a sleeping horse!

Relax your mind — and stay at peace.

It is ridiculous to do things by force – poor horse – it looks ridiculous, it is not a beautiful thing to do things by force.

If you sit relaxed in the right position the rest is easy!

You must know how, but first you must FEEL. If you know all things and have no feel – that is a disaster. In training a horse, a rider cannot have only one system because each horse is different.

Thousands of little things – all must be remembered by the rider. One must never cease to observe each horse.

When one speaks of impulsion to the riders they have a tendency to push or rush, when one speaks of lightness they have a tendency to abandon.

The rider who all his life looks for the best sensations or feelings from his horse, and, who each time looks for his own feelings and thoughts on each and every occasion to be more in harmony.

The man who does all this knows well that each horse is different from every other horse.

The horse is not a machine, it is a living being. Of course one rides him and he never forgets the movements he has learned, but what is necessary to know is to ask the commands correctly, without bad consequences to the body of the horse.

To reduce to the minimum the problems and resistances, which occur during training a horse, it is necessary for the rider to have patience, gentleness and some intelligence.

First a relaxed mind...then a relaxed horse.

Doctors, lawyers and businessmen think with their heads. Riders must learn to think with their bottoms!

The rider must pay basic attention to the horse's calmness, relaxation, straightness, cadence, energy and promptness to the response to the aids.

To return always to the basic exercises and to spend more time with them than with the more advanced exercises. These advanced exercises one asks for at a time when one feels the horse is ready to perform them.

It is better to do them little and well than many times and often not well.

To know and understand that the spur is not always the expression of the strength of the leg but, also perhaps is an aid for relaxation and calmness of the horse.

The tactful rider feels if part of the horse is tired and knows how to help the horse to engage this part without force.

It is always necessary to complete a session of work thinking about the horse being in his best frame of mind the next day.

It is the rider who decides how and in which variation of each pace he must work the horse. The final result must be good for the rider and for the horse, and not always for the judges or the spectators sitting on chairs.

If you move your body more than the back of the horse, there is no co-operation between you and the horse.

More often than not it is we ourselves who keep a horse from performing a movement correctly because of the rider's incorrect use of aids and a poor seat.

Observation of the horse, reflection and reading, not only of that which is written today, but also the works of the Old Masters, added to practice will increase your understanding.

Don't get complicated.

THE AIDS — BACK, SEAT, AND WEIGHT

T HE degree of finesse of a horse is directly related to the degree of finesse of the rider's aids. It is ridiculous to do things by force – poor horse – it looks ridiculous. It is not a beautiful thing to do things by force.

He learns – give him a pat.

BACK, SEAT AND WEIGHT

The most important piece the rider has is his back.

If you stay too rigid in the back you take the mouth of the horse.

You must relax your waist and your back to go with the back of the horse and keep your bottom in the saddle.

Body and legs in a straight line.

Relax your waist and let your bottom push the horse.

Do not contract the bottom. Sit straight and open the bottom.

Waist relaxed. If you stay rigid in the waist and use your legs the horse is rigid.

In the canter keep the waist relaxed to keep the bottom in the saddle.

When you do a circle do not sit to the outside, push your bottom a little to the inside. In the turns, influence the horse by your back.

Look to your position at trot.

It is not only to force your shoulders back, this means nothing. The shoulders appear to move back, when the waist moves down and forward.

Do not believe that during the horse's training you might not change your position a little to help him. In some cases, the rider can lighten the horse's

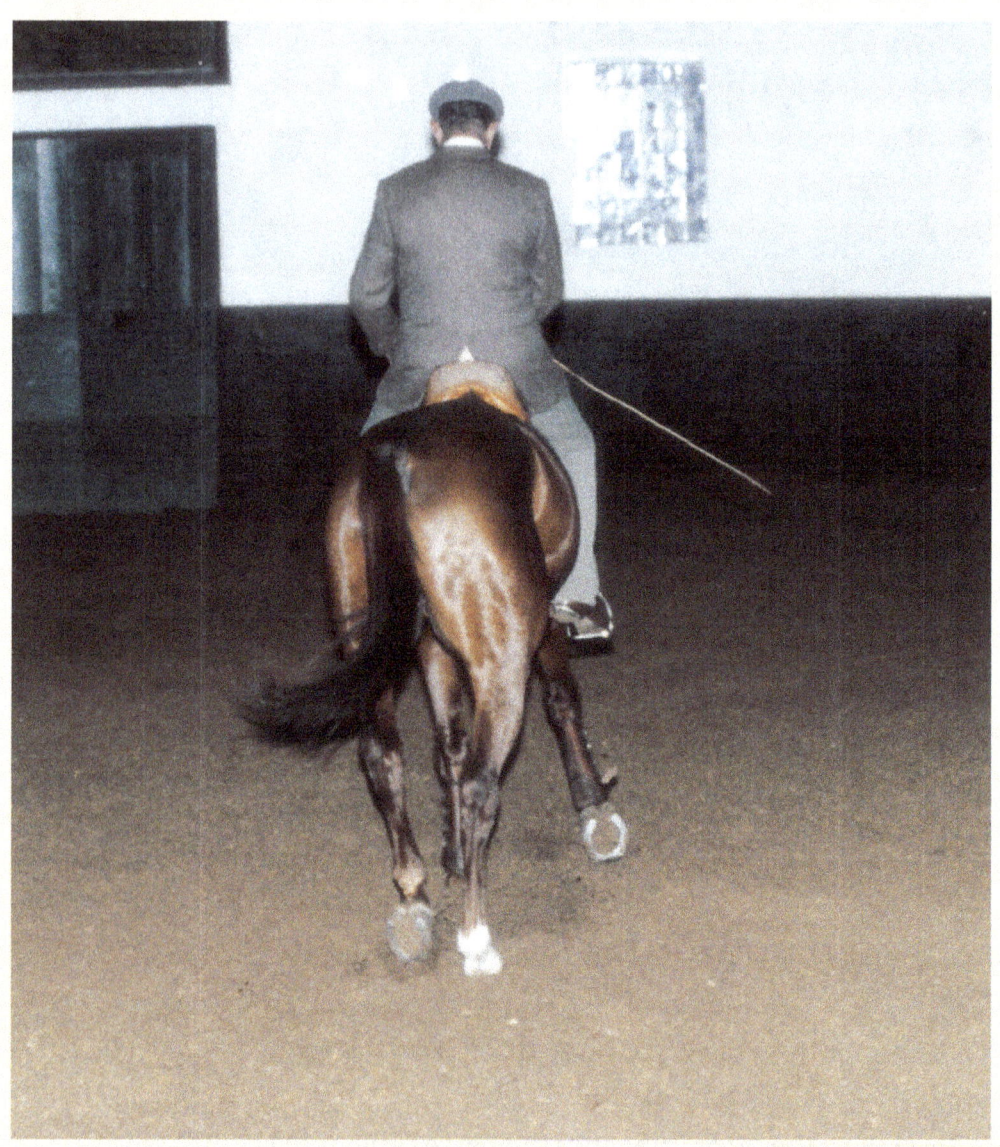

Feel the horse move under your bottom.

hind-quarter, incline himself a little forward, or to lighten the horse's shoulders, incline himself a little backward.

Each of these actions are different, and here, it is the feeling and the rider's ultra-rapid reflexes, which allow that you give the right aid at the precise moment.

Training of horse is above all feeling and trying, according to what you feel, to help the horse and not to force him.

As the horse becomes regular and easy, then the rider can sit very steady but with a relaxed waist.

You must also, sitting straight, be able to sit heavier by relaxing the buttock and having your bottom more open on the saddle, or when you sit lighter then you sit with a more closed bottom.

You must understand the feelings the horse gives you, which make you choose how to sit and when.

Do not move your back more than the back of the horse.

The most important piece a rider has is his back.

THE AIDS — THE RIDER'S LEGS

ONE always speaks about the lightness of the rider's hands but one forgets to speak about the lightness of the action of the rider's legs.

If the legs act through pressure what happens? At first, the rider, through this pressure contracts the muscles of his thighs and his back and then his whole body will become stiff.

Secondly, he must not forget that the horse breathes and when the rider's legs are fixed then the horse's breathing is constricted.

You must not forget that with the legs pressuring the horse, the rider does not have a correct contact in the hand because the hand receives the faults of the legs.

The legs of the rider must remain near the horse's sides but freely relaxed, able to give gentle touches with the calf of the leg. It is important to know how to use the spur by relaxing the ankle and to know whether and when the spur is in contact with the horse's side, or not.

Develop subtle aids which allow the rider who knows these aids to ride his horse more easily than the rider who uses his legs badly. The latter leads to the horse working with dullness and confusion.

Allow the legs to touch and then relax, without displacing the legs and as quickly as possible. Learn also to leave the legs in contact, completely relaxed, feeling the sides of the horse without pressure. Be able to round your legs around the horse to be able to use the spur without the leg.

It is all these subtle aids, which allow the rider who knows them to ride his horse more easily than the one who uses his legs badly. The latter leads the horse finally to confusion and the rider's legs are incapable of making the laziest of horses alert. The rider who uses his legs correctly and with tact can ride any sort of horse.

Practice shows us that a horse cannot give you his back without being curved (laterally) around the rider's inside leg.

Practice shows us that a horse cannot give you his back without being curved (laterally) around the rider's inside leg.

The rider who turns the horse's head to the inside without first relaxing the inside curve of his horse's body only achieves a twisted and resisting position of the horse's head.

It is the rider's inside leg which is active, and what is necessary is that the horse turns around the rider's inside leg without having any extra weight on either the inside shoulder or outside shoulder.

A big mistake that many riders do is to use too much inside leg in the canter. The resultant difficulties come from the fact that they have not first in-curved the horse around their inside leg, and they use this leg with touches which are equal to the touches of the outside leg when cantering – this, the horse does not understand and the result is confusion in the horse's mind.

Again about the legs of the rider I would like to say...

>They push...They calm...

>>They put between...

>>>They...relax the horse.

One must always be careful about the amount of action of the legs in relation to the amount of action of the hands.

If the legs are sufficient then use only the legs but if they are not sufficient then use the spurs with moderation and tact.

To know and understand the spur is not always the expression of the strength of the leg but, also, perhaps as an aid for the relaxation and calmness of the horse

The rider's legs must relax close around the horse's sides without any muscular contraction, which will make for supple application of the rider's legs when needed, to which the horse can respond smoothly without rigidity or harshness, or even rejection of the action of the rider's legs.

THE AIDS — SPURS / RIDER'S HANDS

SPURS

So you need to put the toe of your foot down a little, and with the heel supple, the spur arrives on the horse as the fingers of a guitarist playing his instrument.

THE HANDS OF THE RIDER

The harmony of the aids! The hand of the rider must feel the horse without him pulling on the hand, but also without pulling in the horse's mouth (head) towards the rider's hand.

Keep the hands quiet and receive the mouth of the horse.

The mouth of the horse and good hands speak constantly.

When you take, take more by your back than by your hands.

To take – the closing of the fingers with a still hand, the result of the arm, suitably placed with elbows near the body, the flexion of the waist and the position of the chest all suitably relaxed.

"GIVE" is not to drop the reins, but go/move/proceed with much less, sometimes without weight in the reins or the shoulders.

I do not say drop the reins, but see if the horse goes without any weight in the reins.

If the hands are too strong you block the movement. Riders with too much weight in the reins cause their horses to put too much weight onto the horse's shoulders.

A simple snaffle can be a very hard bit when a horse is fighting against it, and a double bridle can be very soft if it is used with an experienced hand, and the horse 'gives' under the action of that experienced hand.

You need to put the toe of your foot down a little, and, with the heel supple the spur arrives on the horse like the fingers of a guitarist playing his instrument.

Do not believe that during the horse's training you may not change your position a little to help him.

In some cases, to lighten the horse's shoulders, a rider can incline himself a little backwards...

The hand which is not experienced but only good is very often wrong, and with sensations of untrue lightness those untrue sensations come from the tongue that is not quietly in its place but comes up, sometimes in a ball and sometimes comes over the bit.

I feel a great rage when I am told that the horse must be permanently against the bit as it is the only way to vary the speed of the movement or, also, it is the only way to keep a horse straight.

I believe that there should never be any confusion in the rider's understanding of the difference between this heavy contact in the rider's hand, and the necessary light, sensitive contact, which activates the reins. This latter feeling gives sensitivity to the rider, which clearly results in sensitive horses.

This harmony is dressage for the elite.

Someone says, "take hold of the reins and do not lose the contact with the reins."

Someone else says, "give the rein as much as possible so as to give the horse the habit to work free, happy, and light."

Of course there is a little of the truth in both cases, but especially what you must know, is when to keep the contact and when you must give the contact.

The time to keep the contact can arrive at a different moment according to the horse you work. You must first know the degree of desire of the horse himself to go forward, the nervous system of this particular horse, the origin of the rigidity or stiffness, or his one-sidedness.

The action/the feeling to the rider in the hands should resemble a filter. Excessive force, pulling by the arm muscles of the rider will never give the horse an air of elegance, fluidity or grace.

Do not forget all persons have a tendency to have more force (strength) in one side more than the other.

I suggest you attach the reins to a wall and take the reins in both hands as is normal nowadays. Measure the pressure of each hand (rein) with a small scale for weighing and afterwards, remember and understand the difference in your hands.

With reins too long – it is very nice to do little movements with the reins very long, but if the horse jumps you take the mouth of the horse.

With reins too short you contract the body of the horse. The more you make the direction by your legs the less you need the hands.

How much simpler it is if the rider does not do lots of things with the hands?

You keep the contact not because you take the mouth of the horse but because you have the rein in the right position.

Do not let the horse sleep on your hands.

Never press (push) only with the legs.

Work more by the back.

Work more by the legs than by the hands.

Resist, do not pull, when the head is in the wrong position and "GIVE" when the horse gives.

If the horse moves his head, push, back and legs, and 'fix' the hands, give when the horse gives.

Sit forward, see if your hands are moving because the reins are too short or too long. You cannot control your horse if your hands move constantly.

You keep the contact not because you take the mouth of the horse but because you have the rein in the right position.

The hands they are the last thing, the last aid you use.

...or to lighten the horse's hind quarters, the rider can incline himself a little forward.

HORSES' MOVEMENT

SOME horses born with natural movement, very long, and with a very good natural cadence and most of all with a natural balance, which means under the weight of the rider at the beginning, they keep their natural movement with good balance.

Some others also have good movement but do not have good balance, and with the weight of the rider they begin to lean on the hand of the rider, and put weight on their shoulders.

Some others, because of their conformation, lift their legs too high, stay with the weight behind and do not go forward correctly. Still others, with not enough elevation, take "picky" little steps and stay with the shoulders contracted and un-relaxed.

The horse must learn to be balanced, to be capable of moving in the three paces, in the variations of these paces, shorter or longer, and in the different transitions, between different paces.

First you see how the back moves under the weight of the rider and you decide in which rhythm/cadence you must work.

What I am totally against, is to obtain the development of the movement by work in resistance, which gives the horse the habit to lean on the hand.

Progressively as soon as they find their cadence and are comfortable in this cadence, you can expand the length of the movement.

WALK

It is necessary to walk more actively if the horse does not maintain his rhythm. Walk slowly with power.

Do not let your horse sleep.

Extend your walk by your back and waist and not by your legs.

Relax your hands and allow the horse to move under you.

If your walk is not active, does not go forward, in the transition into trot the horse's head will come up.

TROT

Rising trot until the horse's back is relaxed, then sit, then rise when not relaxed.

The rhythm is a very important point, it must be maintained with power. Do not change the rhythm.

Calm with power.

Many riders use and abuse the working trot too much. There are several nuances of trot which are convenient for one or another trot at this or another level of training. It is the rider who decides how and in which variation of each pace he must work the horse.

The final result must be good for the rider and for the horse, and not always for the judges and spectators sitting on chairs.

Do not lose the trot, relax your hands.

All things in the same trot, same rhythm.

By sitting collect the trot, think of the rhythm and lightness.

Relax in the trot before cantering. Put your horse forward in trot then canter.

If you let the horse sleep in the trot he will play in the canter.

CANTER

Canter when the horse is not resisting.

Before collection, develop the habit of doing transitions and cantering in the natural balance. Not collected by the reins.

Do thousands of transitions without weight in the reins. Trot, canter, trot, and canter in self-carriage.

Horses come to collection more easily and quicker if, in the beginning, the canter is relaxed and in the natural balance. They accept the collection without force.

When the horse is confident in his balance in his free canter, he is ready to begin to reduce the canter and to carry himself on his hindquarters and, also to go from a walk to a canter.

Most riders begin straight away the beginnings of departure from walk to canter. It is easy for the horse to begin through the transition from a very collected trot to the canter.

Out of the collected trot we try to achieve several strides of a collected canter, before allowing the horse to relax and come back easily to a walk.

When the horse is able to sustain the collected canter to the walk easily, (certain horses lose the impulsion more quickly than others and others get more excited at the effort made through the hindquarters) you can begin to ask for the transition from canter to walk.

It is necessary to be very attentive to the action of the back of the rider, one must return again to the walk through the use of the back and chest of the rider.

The horse must learn to come to a collected walk while remaining light. It is in the perfection of the transition from the canter to the walk that one finds one of the great secrets to the subsequent success with the flying changes.

A horse does not develop balance and collection in canter by cantering for a long time – but by the frequent transitions to the canter from the halt, walk and trot. Variations in the length of stride and the collection assist in developing a correct collected canter.

COUNTER CANTER

Counter canter is physically difficult and should not be over done. Most of all it is difficult for the young horse and care should be taken not to ask for too much.

If he changes legs while at counter canter he must be brought back to walk, collected, asked again to strike off in counter canter. Fairly frequent rewards of walk on long reins in the middle of these counter canters will help the horse.

When he can maintain the counter canter down the long side he can begin a large circle of counter canter.

The horse must be straight on the circle in counter canter.

The counter canter is a good exercise to help improve the cadence of the gait, makes it more active, more round, and increases the impulsion, while remaining straight.

The horse must be straight on the circle in counter canter.

FLYING CHANGES

The secret of good flying changes are the transitions from canter to walk. Keep the horse straight. Do not let the horse put the weight in the shoulders or shoulder, keep the horse straight.

The horse must be straight, during and after the flying change.

Keep the rhythm. Do not let the horse change the rhythm.

Look if the horse keeps the same rhythm after the change.

The aid is an electric touch, not a strong push.

So many times I have seen a horse ready to give his first flying change easily and his rider, instead of asking with tact, has given the aids too strongly, so that the horse remembers and remains excited each time that he thinks one is going to ask him for a flying change.

Or, as with certain horses, they remain for a long time nervous each time they pass the place where the demand was made.

As the changes become more easy, you can ask them in different places, always calmly and in the same cadence. Progressively you can ask more, say, four and then six changes.

When you begin to ask the change on the diagonal it is of utmost importance to look straight to the spot where the horse will arrive at the other long side, and not let the weight of the horse be more on one shoulder of the horse than the other.

Before beginning the timed flying changes it is necessary to do single changes on the short side, on the circles, in both directions and on both reins.

The progress must be slow and you must remember this when you start to ask, for example, for a flying change every fourth stride. It is necessary that during the steps between the two flying changes that the rider reinforces the aids of that canter in which the horse goes. Those aids will imperceptibly confirm the canter with each step, reversing the aids at the precise moment of the second flying change.

An error I see most riders commit is not keeping the outside rein still.

Do not forget it is the outside rein which keeps the collection of the canter, and the best way of maintaining the horse's cadence is for the rider to put his shoulder from that side slightly further back.

Come back to collected trot from the extended trot more by your back than by your hands.

Most of all in the flying change sit still. If you must move your bottom in the flying change then you would be better to go to a discotheque!

EXTENDED TROT

The only true extension of the trot is the one, which is the result of collection with the horse light and on his hindquarters.

The lengthening of the trot with showy movements of the shoulders in which the back of the horse remains hollow and the hind legs are left behind, and sometimes spread apart, does not figure in the domain of equestrian art.

It is always necessary during a lengthening to think of returning to collected trot, with a lowering of the hindquarters and in lightness, and not to throw the horse onto the shoulders with one or two rigid steps.

In the extended trot, the degree of impulsion enables the horse to take advantage of a yielding rein to cover the ground in balance.

When taking the diagonal, you must watch that the weight does not come onto the inside shoulder. This is a reason that one must remember that the correct riding of each corner is a small moment of the Shoulder-In.

If the lengthening is obtained, after having acquired collection and cadence, the horse has a supple back and the rider can sit without moving in the saddle, and without bouncing as one often sees in lengthenings that are prematurely requested.

At extended trot do not let the horse put the head low. Young or green horses yes, but advanced horses no, because they move in collection.

Come back from extended trot to collected trot more by your back than by your hands.

WORK WITH THE LUNGE

FREE lunge to allow the horse to loosen his muscles.

Sometimes a horse sleeps with a kink in his back – you should think of this!

I speak about the rider who uses the lunge to warm up his horse or to position his horse using a gadget.

It must be the rider who lunges the horse not somebody else. Later the way he rides the horse must be influenced, must be the result of what he sees while watching the horse working on the lunge.

He must look at…

a) The attitude/movement of the horse's back.

b) Position of the neck and watch the muscles of the neck.

c) Rhythm in all gaits.

d) The difference between horses, that are, "hot" and "cold." Some horses need to work with the head a little higher or a little lower.

e) How to attach and adjust each rein correctly, that is, how long to have them. This knowledge comes from observing the whole horse in movement, and not only the appearance of the head and neck, but remember to watch the whole body of the horse and especially the way the hindquarters move in rhythm.

At the beginning, you must avoid shortening the side reins too much; this will bring the horse's neck into a position that would not be in harmony with the rest of his body.

Shortening of the side reins, too much and too quickly hollows the horse's back and results in not allowing the horse's back to move normally in a rounded manner.

Free lunge to allow your horse to loosen his muscles.

Always, a reward.

We must keep the horse on a correct circle by pushing with the whip and by using the elastic tension of the lunge—taking and giving the lunge line. If we allow him to lean to the inside of the circle, and fall in, we are giving him a bad lesson.

We can create many good things with good work on the lunge, and also many bad things which can remain with the horse all his life.

When we work on the lunge, we must change direction on the circle very often.

Some horses need quite long work at lunge with gadgets.

Some others when they have taken the desired position stay there quite easily, and I can not understand why you continue to use the gadgets.

You must never forget that when one lunges a horse that the lunge rein is equivalent to the rein when the rider is on his back, and that the lunge whip is equivalent to the rider's legs. The circle we ask must be a correct geometric circle.

The halt on the lunge, must be asked for very gently by the whip, which shows itself very delicately behind, and with very little vibrations of the lunge, and helped by the voice which is also important.

Here too, in working at the lunge with gadgets it is very important to walk the horse very often to allow the horse to continue to find his own cadence. To carry himself and to lighten himself by this walking so he can proceed in another gait.

Working on the lunge with a horse whose gadget is fitted correctly and in a correct cadence can be a precious aid in training horses.

You must not forget that when you want to make a request or an impression on the cavesson, on the bridge of the horse's nose, it is not by pulling that you will obtain a good result, but it is giving lightly with the lunge, and also to be able to vibrate the lunge.

The gestures of the hand which holds the whip must be restrained and calculated so as the horse gets the habit, progressively, to see the whip without being afraid.

Observe the whole horse in movement, and not just the look of the head and neck. Always remember the whole body of the horse and especially the way the hindquarters move in rhythm.

On a young horse, give the inside rein during the canter transition.

He learns... give him a pat.

YOUNG HORSES

HE learns...give him a pat.

Horses must learn to stand very quiet on a loose rein.

Stay quiet at halt. This is very important.

Make the horse your friend, not a slave and you will have a friend for all his life.

When you are working a young horse carry the whip on the inside.

Let the neck and head extend at halt and see if the back of the horse is relaxed and the horse looks towards the floor.

If the horse's head is too low in the beginning – by the impulsion the head will come to a correct position.

The horse cannot learn with the head and neck in the air. Horses come without force or traction. Play with the reins, make the poll round by "playing" – not by force.

Riders with too much weight in the reins cause their horses to put too much weight in the shoulders.

Young horses must trot, canter, trot, canter...in self-carriage, not by the assistance of the reins.

On a young horse, give the inside rein during the canter transition.

The horse cannot be forward if not relaxed in body and mind.

A calm horse is not a sleeping horse.

Do not let your horse sleep on your hands.

RELAXATION OF THE HORSE

To lengthen or extend the horse's neck you must ask slowly and progressively and, do not allow the horse to lengthen his neck, by himself or quickly.

To do this slowly and softly is the proof of a relaxed and round back.

If you give the reins and the horse does not extend his neck then you can be sure you have not worked the horse correctly; you have put your horse into collection in a bad position, by the opposing forces of the hands and legs.

If the horse is not capable of extending his neck in all three paces and staying in the rhythm, the cadence of the gait, with his back round, then you can be sure the work you do is not correct.

Sometimes when you (the rider) thinks the horse is light, balanced, cadenced in collection, you can ask the horse to lengthen his neck. If he grabs or tugs at the reins or puts his head down quickly then the back will go flat for a moment and then become hollow.

At the halt, an experienced rider with a correctly-trained horse can ask for lengthening of the neck. The horse will stay quiet and correct at halt while he lengthens his neck, and he will return to the previous flexion at the halt without moving his legs.

Do not forget there is a relation between all the muscles of the whole body of the horse.

Let your horse look towards the floor and follow his back with your back.

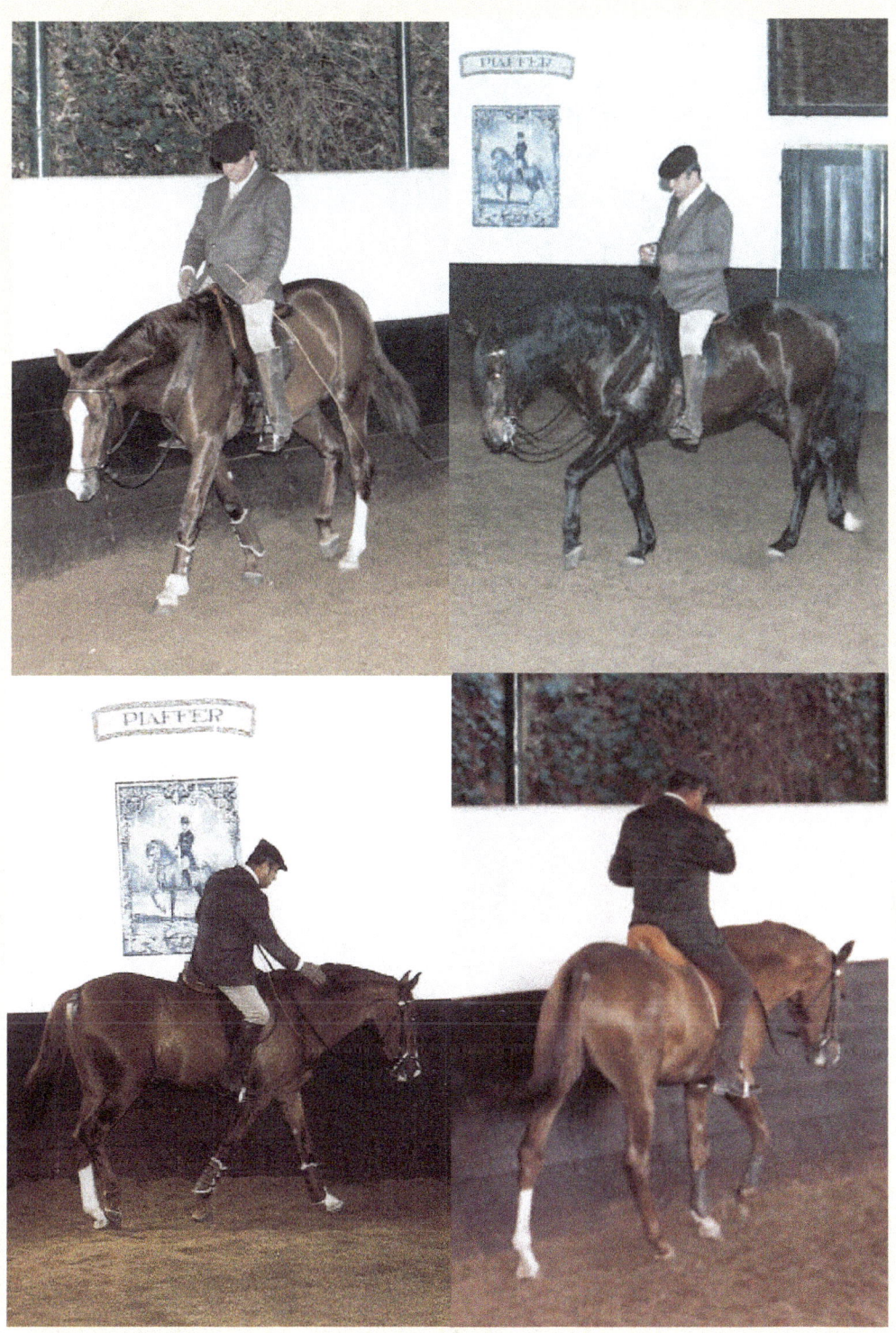

Let your horse look towards the floor and follow his back with your back.

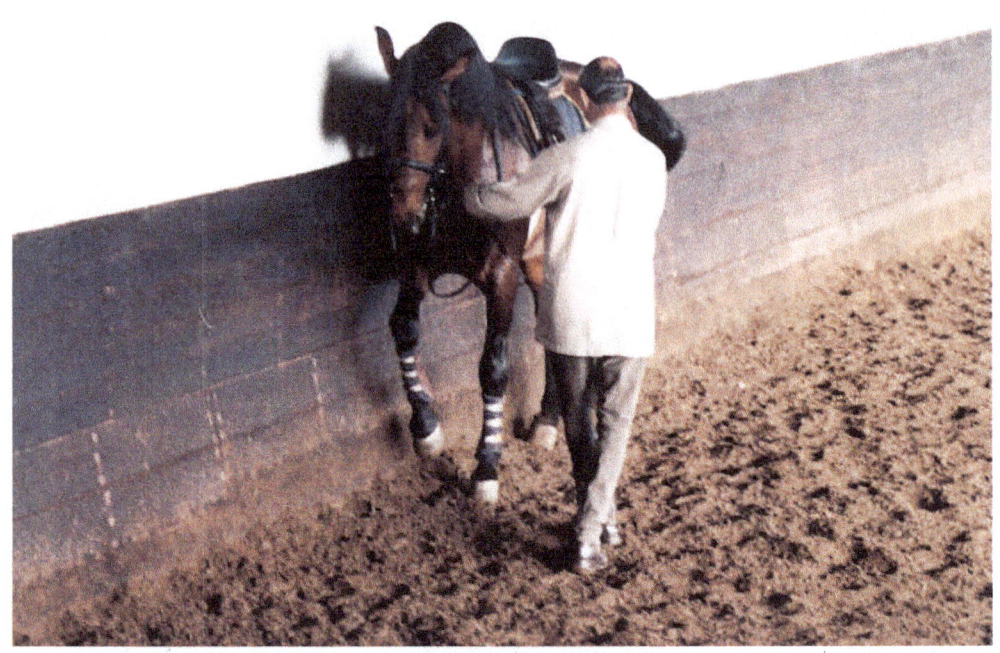

To ask for the rein back is by a touch of the rider's legs followed by the rider's back and fingers on the rein.

HALT AND REIN BACK

Originally, a 'halt' performed with a young horse was called a 'stop'. The prime importance was that the horse stand calm and immobile, which would also achieve his mental relaxation. It was not expected to be a square halt.

It takes tact and patience to teach a nervous or irritable horse to stand immobile. A horse which is trained should be able to stand motionless and not move until his rider asks him to regardless of other noises, movements, or any other distractions. To accomplish this, the rider needs a great deal of patience and the horse needs many rewards.

To ask for the halt the rider uses his weight and his buttocks and back to sit more deeply in the saddle. His hands are the last aid and when the horse halts the rider should relax his fingers to maintain only a soft contact so that the horse does not drop his head.

As the horse's training progresses by asking some halts during Shoulder-In and travers, the horse will begin to halt more rounded, then the halt will become more square.

This halt should not be with rigid legs, but instead, the rider should feel in the saddle a gentle lowering of the horse's hindquarters. It should not be a hurried or abrupt feeling.

When the horse will stop square on his hindquarters lightly from a walk or trot, and moves forward in the same walk or trot, light, and without altering his head or neck, it is time to start to ask for the rein back.

REIN BACK

Asking for the rein back is done by a touch of the rider's legs followed by the rider's back and his fingers on the reins. When the horse gives the first beginning of a step back the rider immediately drops the reins, rewards him and allows him to freely walk forward.

If a horse puts his hind quarters to either side during a rein back, it's by using the opposite rein to put the shoulders in the same line as the hind quarters that one straightens him.

If the rein back is badly executed or anticipated or if the horse runs back, then the horse has learned a dangerous evasion. To stop this, the horse must be stopped, walked a few steps forward and again asked to step slowly and calmly in rein back.

Later, from the walk, halt, then rein back two or three steps and go forward in the same gait.

Later do the same at trot. It is very important in these two exercises at the walk and trot that the rein back be easy and slow and that the horse is prompt to move forward from the halt.

A good solution to the training difficulty of a horse which tends to be heavy on the forehand or sleeping on the bit, is this method of calm rein back repeated and performed without haste and with equal steps.

CIRCLES

WHEN I work my horses, it is rare that I do not begin by asking for little circles in both directions at the walk before I ask for anything else.

When the horse is accepting the inside leg in both directions, you need only to use the same inside leg with little touches if you begin to feel the horse becoming contracted, stiff, or leaning on the inside shoulder.

The circle is of utmost importance especially in a young horse

The circle must be a perfect geometric figure

When following the curved line of the circle, the horse must adapt his spine – the whole of his spinal column, to the line of the circle.

When I work my horse, I often begin by asking for little circles on each rein at the walk before I ask for anything else.

I also ask for some Shoulder-In on these small circles.

Horses...they learn a lot as they follow the correct line of the circle.

CIRCLES / SERPENTINES

On the circle establish rhythm, impulsion, position.

A circle is not a potato or an egg.

All the body of the horse must stay on the line of the circle.

Horses, they learn a lot as they follow the correct line of the circle.

The corner, the circle and the Shoulder-In are a *"ménage à trois."*

Working the horse in canter on circles is one of the most successful ways to give him suppleness, regularity and balance in this gait.

The circle activates the horse, places his hind legs under him with the resultant improvement in his balance.

SERPENTINES

Ride a serpentine with your legs, not with your hands.

Working the horse in canter on circles is one of the most successful ways to give him suppleness, regularity and balance in this gait.

Class at Avessada, Portugal riding a Serpentine.

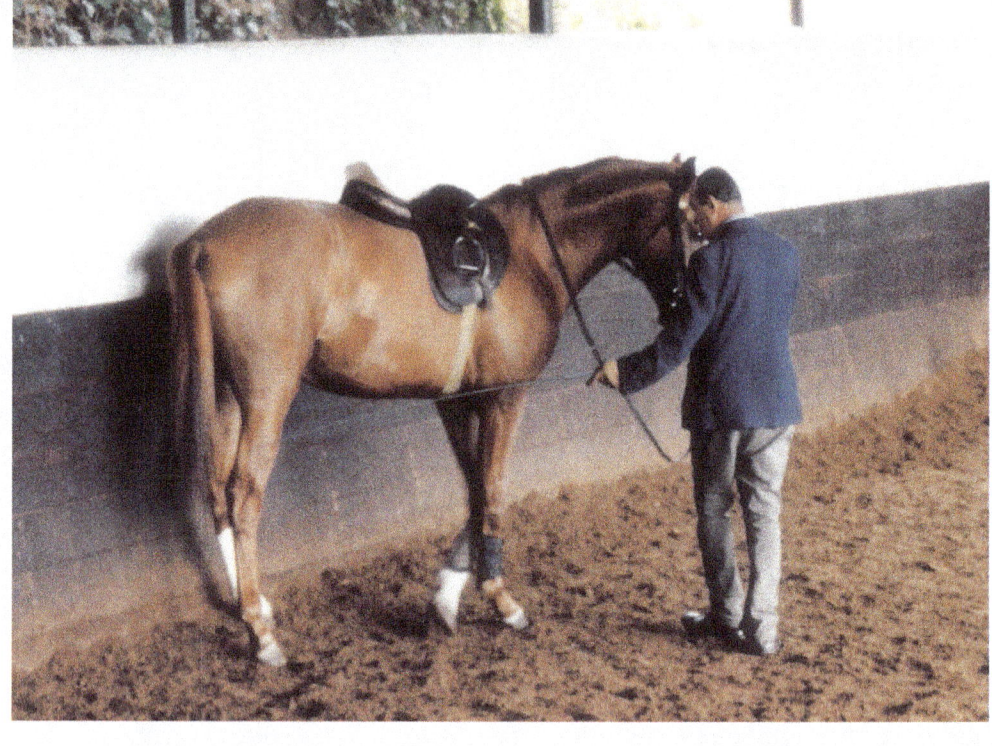

Do not surprise your horse with your aids.

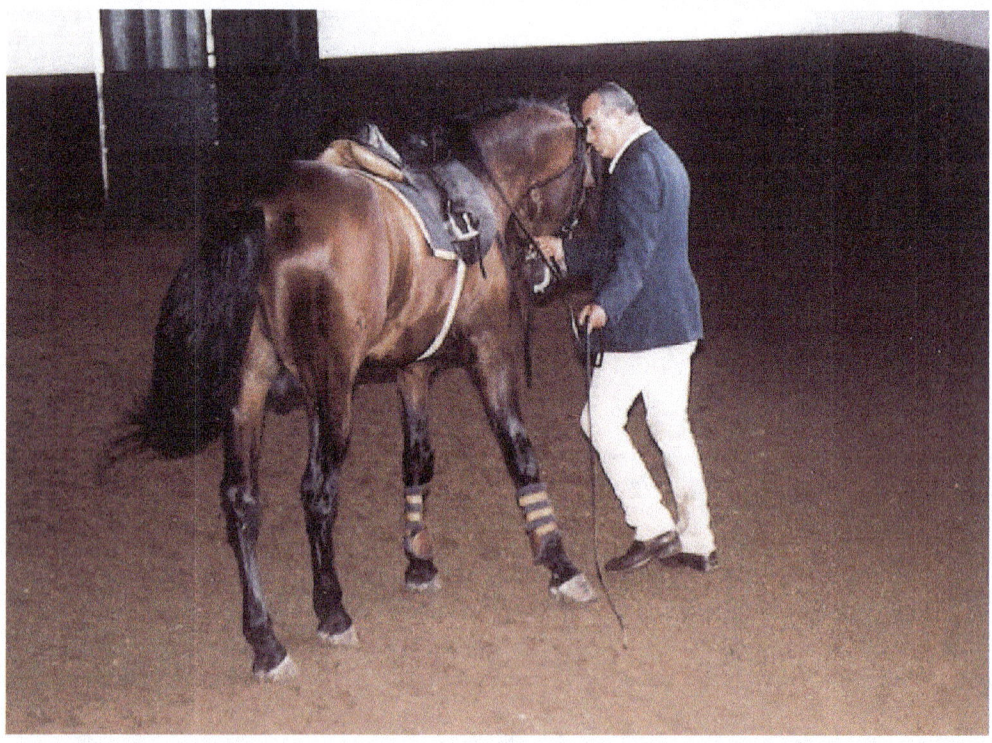

BEGINNING SHOULDER-IN

FOR a young horse that does not know Shoulder-In, this is how one should start.

On a corner of the track, begin to make a correct circle at walk.

Pay attention to the geometry of the circle that it is round and that you do not do it by the backward movement of the inside hand.

The circle must be made in the second half of the short side, going into the corner, and including the beginning of the long side.

When one has obtained a correct circle in a consistent rhythm, on reaching the corner, both hands which are holding the reins very lightly, move slightly to the outside and come back to the inside, while at the same time the inside leg touches at each step, a leg that touches lightly and gives.

Do not surprise the horse with your aids.

IN HAND, by light taps with the whip on the thigh, make him move his hind legs and body one step to the side. Pat him and loosen the rein.

Go very progressively and slowly until the horse begins to give two or three steps sideways easily. When he gives them well to both sides put him straight to the wall and, in making him go forward, imperceptibly bent to the inside, one begins with the greatest delicacy to try two or three steps of Shoulder-In. Pat him.

Often you halt the horse or stop it in this position of the exercise.

One will begin later to ask the horse to make the corners in Shoulder-In, taking care the hind legs walk more and the front legs less so that the angle is the same on the next side. Reward him.

SHOULDER-IN

NUNO Oliveira often quoted de la Guérinière...

"The Shoulder-In is the first and the last lesson to give to a horse."

The Shoulder-In is a major exercise in suppleness. It must be performed and asked for correctly, otherwise it is as one often sees, a horse walking sideways in a twisted manner which, instead of making the horse supple throws his weight onto the outside shoulder.

Shoulder-In is the exercise to use in order to increase the engagement of the hindquarters. It is of less importance for the horse to walk sideways than it is important for him to bend along the whole of his body.

You must not achieve this by force.

It is important to feel that the horse carries himself, that he is not over-bent in the neck, and that he puts his weight onto the inside hind leg and not on the outside shoulder.

Correctly done the Shoulder-In gives great results as it relaxes and straightens the horse.

But one should say shoulders-In not Shoulder-In, because the two shoulders are in, one slightly more that the other.

When walking, one must always be aware that the horse is performing the Shoulder-In with slow strides and not hurried. Nor in a very wide step, because owing to the mechanism of the walk, if the strides are long the back of the horse grows hollow.

I never begin the training of a horse by giving him a lesson other than Shoulder-In. This gymnastic exercise results in the correct lowering of the hind quarters and causes the forehand to raise and lighten, never the opposite.

The Shoulder-In is the first and the last lesson to give to a horse.

The Shoulder-In is a major exercise in suppleness.

Begin the Shoulder-In energetically, do not begin sleeping, but not in a big walk. If you do the horse will hollow his back, a shorter walk is correct.

If the hands are too strong they block the movement. If you pull the inside rein you break the neck.

Often, riders begin the exercise of Shoulder-In incorrectly by activating the inside rein.

In Shoulder-In make sure you sit in the middle of the horse, that you do not lean to the inside or the outside.

In Shoulder-In you must feel that the power comes from the inside leg.

When the horse has given one or two steps of a beginning of Shoulder-In, one drops the reins and pats him. One begins again, until little by little the horse increases the number of steps.

Reward often, ask only a little each time, reward a lot.

When the horse begins to give progressively more steps on the long side, this is the moment that the rider must see that the horse's weight remains on the inside hind leg and not on the outside shoulder.

Later, when the young horse knows a little of the Shoulder-In attention must be given, when one begins, to the outside rein which must act first in order to bring the horse's shoulders to the inside and then the inside rein gives the flexion.

The Shoulder-In exercise is easy to execute if you start delicately. If you push too much the horse will resist.

When the horse executes the Shoulder-In correctly at walk without difficulty, it is time to ask for it at trot.

Between requests for the Shoulder-In at walk, sometimes reward the horse with a long rein. At other times put him into trot making sure he remains straight through the departure.

Look at the so-called Shoulder-In so often seen, in which the rider pulls on the inside rein, leans to the same side, with his leg drawn back to spur the poor animal which forces the horse to move while remaining twisted, taking away all impulsion from the horse, leading to his resistance against the rider.

Many riders make Shoulder-In when they are not well prepared. I would call these badly done contortions, and it would be better not to use this bad contortion of Shoulder-In. It would be more useful if one cannot execute a

Shoulder-In correctly, to stay in the very simple work of circles, well done geometrically.

The bend of a horse is something natural. We can bend the horse very well and very badly.

What you must do is to use it well and usefully.

The Shoulder-In you execute in competition must be in accord with the definitions of the Federation Equestre Internationale.

But the Shoulder-In in which you work your horse at different levels of dressage is conditioned by the needs useful to that horse at that stage of his suppleness.

If the horse has too much weight on the outside shoulder move your hands lightly to the inside.

If you pull the inside rein you break the neck...relax the inside rein.

Do not block with your hands.

Remember the better the Shoulder-In, the better the Half-Pass!

The Shoulder-In is to improve all things. The walk, the trot, and the canter.

Later when the horse performs the Shoulder-In well at walk down the long sides, start to ask for the Shoulder-In on a large circle, on a half circle and always with the outside rein in order to be able to put him back very straight on the centre line.

At walk it is also very good to ask the horse to halt completely quiet, in the position of Shoulder-In. After a few seconds, begin to move again, maintaining this Shoulder-In position, or put the horse in the position of the opposite Shoulder-In and move off.

A very important point is that before asking for a Shoulder-In at trot, the rider establishes and keeps the rhythm of the trot, so that when asking for Shoulder-In, the horse stays in the rhythm of the trot that has been established. All this must be carried out making certain that the hind quarters remain near the wall.

I would like to say that when one walks straight in a manège each corner is a small moment of Shoulder-In and you must not forget that the manège has four corners.

HALF-PASS

WHEN the horse knows well the exercise of Shoulder-In and, having been prepared with the Shoulder-In exercise, has a certain roundness, then he is ready to begin the Half-Pass.

Through the Shoulder-In he has also learned (if the rider paid attention to having his legs in contact) to move away from the leg when touched.

Here is how to begin Half-Pass...

Begin the Shoulder-In in the middle of the long side and continue as far as the middle of the short side in Shoulder-In, turn down the centre line in the position of that Shoulder-In and in this position proceed a little without altering the position of the inside aids.

Apply the outside leg (behind the girth) lightly and with little touches push the horse in the same bend sideways in the position of Half-Pass for two or three steps. Relax the reins and reward the horse. Only ask him to do a few steps at a time and reward him frequently.

This is an important detail: when you take the centre line and when you advance in the position of Shoulder-In the inside leg pushes the hindquarters very slightly to the outside, the outside rein then sends the shoulders in the direction of the Half-Pass, all this in the moment you advance. The body of the horse is in the angle of the Half-Pass and the horse performs the Half-Pass more easily.

To increase little by little the number of steps, pay attention that when the horse is in Half-Pass, in the moment that the horse gives and goes in Half-Pass, the inside leg becomes the most important aid.

Begin the Half-Pass around your inside leg.

Control the Half-Pass with your inside leg and outside rein. In Half-Pass try to arrive at the long side with more inside leg. Finish the Half-Pass with more inside leg than outside, this proves the impulsion.

Begin the Half-Pass around your inside leg.

In the Half-Pass the inside leg gives the flexion. Get the flexion first then use the outside leg.

Be very attentive to your inside leg.

You must touch with one leg and stay quiet with the other or the horse will become confused.

In the beginning to do Shoulder-In and Half-Pass you must touch for one step only to allow the horse to step without being in a hurry. In most cases it happens that we press all the time and not always at a good time. That is the reason we see insufficient crossing of the horse's legs. We do not allow the horse the time to do the movement in cadence.

The horse moves from left to right, he must keep the same bend that he would have when doing a right Shoulder-In, and he must advance bending to the right, shoulders slightly, very slightly ahead of the hindquarters as a result of the action of the left/outside rein. The rider's right/inside leg maintains the impulsion and the bend to the right with the help of a 'giving' inside/right rein. The horse must keep the same angle with which he began, during the entire exercise.

The rider's outside leg stays in the same place as it was during Shoulder-In, that is, a little further back than the inside leg, and should intervene to give impulsion if the hind quarters become lazy.

Acting in the region of the girth, the inside leg has a spasmodic effect which gives the horse the tendency to turn his head in that direction. However, the inside leg is not only essential to maintain the bend but also the forward movement of the Half-Pass. The feeling of the inside rein must be lighter than the outside rein so that the horse can increase the steps sideways.

Later he will arrive at the long side more supported by the outside rein and the inside leg. This is how you teach the horse to Half-Pass without the head tilted.

Look to your horse's head to see if it is straight.

Each time the horse wants to lead with his hind Quarters-Instead of his shoulders, it is the action of the outside rein, in the direction of the Half-Pass which sends the shoulders more sideways.

Each time that the hind quarters do not move actively enough sideways it is the opening of the outside rein in the opposite direction that corrects that tendency. The inside rein remains tranquil and through its association with the inside leg (kept in the region of the girth) maintains the bend.

As in Shoulder-In occasionally relax the reins after obtaining two or three steps of correct Half-Pass and at other times trot on.

When the horse knows how to execute well these movements of Half-Pass, start to bend him around your inside leg on a corner and with his head towards the wall, but looking down the track, and his quarters off the track ask for a few steps of Half-Pass.

This movement is called "Travers." When the horse begins to execute the Travers easily, ask him to halt in the position of the exercise (Travers). The horse remains quiet and calm, and from the halt and in the same angle start the Travers again.

Sometimes ask the Travers on the other side of the manège and therefore on the other rein. Take care to keep the horse's shoulder close to the wall.

When the horse is capable of returning to the long side from the centre line maintaining the Half-Pass position while keeping the same angle and the same bend, he is then ready to begin Half-Pass from the long side to the centre line and to continue straight along the centre line.

In the corner, maintain the bend and advance two or three steps with that bend, observing the same aids and precautions as when initially doing the Half-Pass from the centre line.

The rider in all these exercises must be sure that his body does not lean to the outside or to the inside but the rider's weight must remain on the centre of the horse. To avoid the body leaning to the outside, sit down on the inside seat bone.

Half-Pass allows the horse to achieve maximum suppleness and engagement. The degree of bend depends on the conformation of the horse. The bigger the horse, the more bend that is necessary.

When the horse knows these different sorts of Half-Pass, one begins to ask counter changes of hand. Half-Pass from the beginning of the long side to the centre line and on reaching it, return to the same long side at Half-Pass in the opposite direction.

At the moment when one is changing from one direction to the other, it is the inside leg which acts first for two reasons:

The action of the new inside leg towards the girth develops the new bend, and prevents the hindquarters from coming too much to the new direction which makes the horse take the angle of the new direction equal to that of the first.

Look to your horse's head to see if it is straight.

As with Shoulder-In once the horse has executed the exercise at walk, one can then ask him at trot. The rhythm of the trot must be established and maintained in circles, and in Serpentines before one asks for Half-Pass at trot.

When one asks for the Half-Pass at trot, begin from a Shoulder-In, always maintain the same rhythm.

Later, in order to make the horse's back more supple, on a circle make transitions from Shoulder-In to Quarters-In/Travers. Begin at walk. These are excellent exercises.

Having said that Shoulder-In and Half-Pass are two different exercises, I must add that the frequent transitions from one to the other is one of the foundations of good dressage training, making him more relaxed and more receptive.

These gymnastic exercises are important and the more they are followed the more the horse will lighten and the more he will become collected.

In these transitions the horse is bending and straightening without losing any impulsion, changing from one position to the other by the aids which appear to be invisible and without changing the cadence.

In the whole of the horse's training all of the horse's spinal column is worked from between his two ears to his tail.

EYE, MOUTH & JAW

THE EYE OF THE HORSE

The observation of the eye of the horse is very important – one must always make very calm movements which will not frighten the horse.

It is necessary to decide how much relaxation and /or how much stimulation each different horse requires.

If too much either way the horse goes to sleep or he becomes irritable. Riders must not forget to carefully watch the horse's eye with its changing expressions, to read these signs and to use this information to aid in the training.

THE MOUTH OF THE HORSE

The mouth of the horse is one of the most sensitive parts of his body. Nowadays the rider believes that the horse is trained only by the engagement of the hind quarters and that is sufficient to have a good mouth.

Of course we must engage the hind quarters with clever gymnastic exercises, and by the use of these exercises we must activate the hind quarters. But, at the same time, we must understand how the mouth moves and functions.

We must look at the thickness and length of the bars of the mouth, whether they are bony or have plenty of fleshy gums.

Examine the width and depth of the mouth so that you can choose a suitable bit.

Actually, the fashion today is to fasten a dropped noseband very tightly before observing how the mouth moves; this is an error.

As with humans there are some horses which are talkative and some which are mute. We must know how many times we will let the horse chatter since he becomes progressively more attentive and, when he becomes cadenced, and through impulsion, he will stop chattering and will give himself calmly to the different movements we ask of him.

But if we forbid him from chattering, which, of course, we could do by tightening the noseband, what happens?

The horse contracts himself throughout the whole of his head, neck and body, then doesn't relax in the parotid. The muscles of the neck become rigid and the horse becomes rigid in all his body by a general contraction of his muscles. And now here is what ignorant riders say, "at least he is round."

With the mute horse, if we work him in silence we arrive at the same result.

Why is the horse mute[unable to move his mouth]? Because he is in contraction. With a mute horse we must provoke him with clever exercises to attempt to de-contract his jaw.

Do not forget there is a relationship between all of the muscles of the body of the horse.

When must we begin to use a double bridle?

This is a question that many riders ask themselves. Here again there is no one system.

There are some horses who will arrive at the top level still using only a single or snaffle bridle. Some others need a double bridle earlier than this.

Especially we must not forget that the mouth of the horse is placed, like the brain, in his head.

In most cases exercises chosen with wisdom and an experienced hand can solve the problem.

THE JAW OF THE HORSE

Today the rider who feels resistance on one side has a tendency to bring the head to the inside by traction, the horse turns his head because of the strong pull on the rein and appears to give, but then leans on the rein and continues to lean.

This is a bad way, a bad system, and if you repeat this it will continue, and the horse will lean all his life.

Of course the horse stiffened in the jaw, cannot put his weight on the hindquarter.

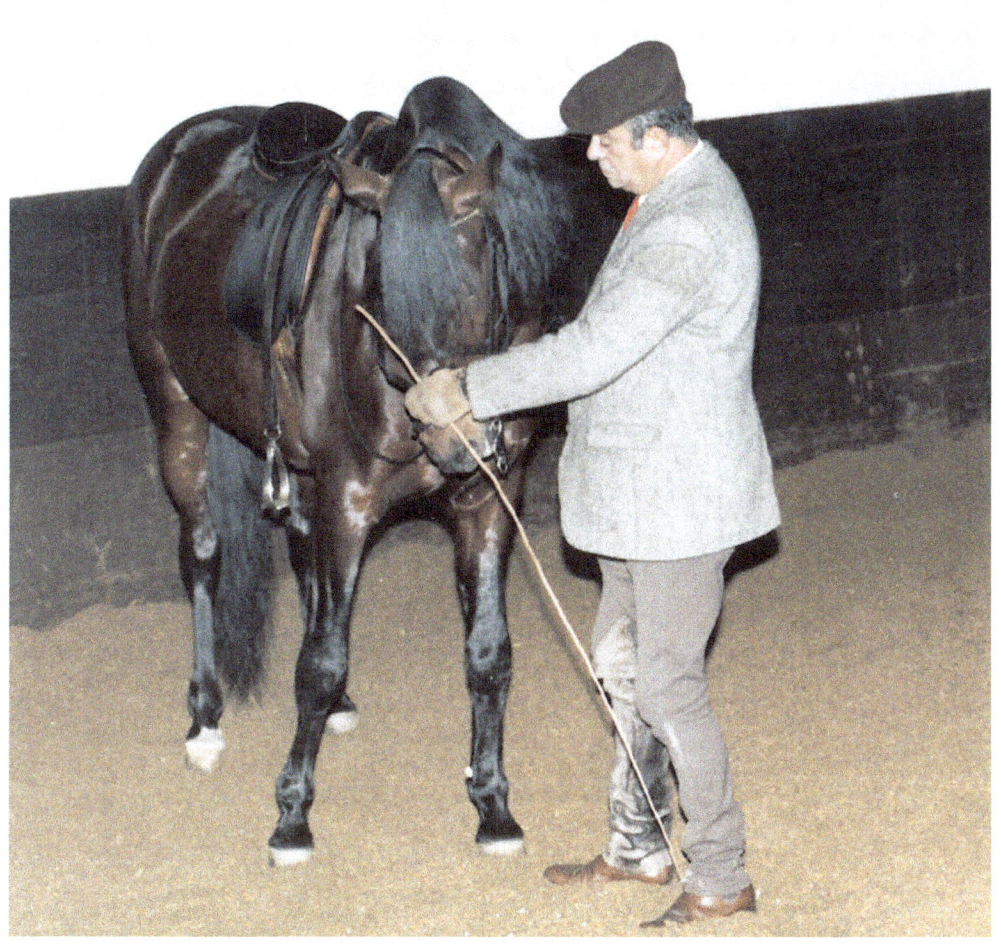

Take care when you do these flexions that the horse does not tilt his head.

But with force he does it by crushing his hindquarters, and so preventing the hindquarters from flexing as they would if he were light in his mouth.

That is the reason why many riders have difficulties in piaffe and pirouette, because the mouth is tightened and the jaw contracted (resisting).

LATERAL FLEXIONS OF THE JAW

The work of the lateral flexions at halt and later, forward is called "to place the horse and flex the horse straight."

If it is done carefully by the action of the legs and the spurs to bring the head laterally, less or more, then the each horse bends laterally more or less depending on their ability.

That flexion which you must obtain with a rein takes a position, but the rein must not be more tense than the rein on the opposite side.

That lateral flexion must be asked for after you have obtained the direct flexion with the lower jaw relaxed and never before. The horse arrives at a point with his head not tilted, but straightened without putting more weight on the inside or the outside shoulder.

When a rider asks for flexions of the jaw either mounted or unmounted, if the horse moves his front legs to the side, this is incorrect.

In lateral flexions the horse must stand square so that no weight falls on either the inside or the outside shoulder.

Take care when you do these lateral flexions that the horse does not tilt his head.

A trained horse must have a neck that is neither too rigid nor too soft.

HORSES THAT MOVE THEIR TAIL

Lots of horses move their tail because of the incorrect actions of the legs or the hands of the rider. Also by the bad way a rider sits on the horse.

For the horse that moves his tail because of a physical problem, it is first a question for the veterinarian, and subsequently by the delicateness of the aiding of the rider that a solution will be arrived at.

I have seen many horses execute many movements that must have been classic if the horse had stayed calm, without excessive movement of the tail, and the eye with an unhappy expression.

These movements you cannot describe as Classical but only as "forced activity."

And when he "gives" you must "give."

CADENCE — IMPULSION

WHAT is cadence? Cadence is rhythm and energy combined, resulting in more suspension in the horse's movements.

This requires muscle tone acquired through the correct, and various supportive exercises during the horse's training.

As the horse remains more round, more receptive, he will be able to pass more easily, more quickly, from one exercise/movement to another, as he begins to collect himself.

Know what the cadence of the collected walk is, what the cadence of the collected trot is, what the cadence of the longer trot is.

It is precisely in the maintenance of the appropriate cadence in each movement that one maintains the lightness, the weight on the haunches and one achieves collection.

When the horse finds his confidence, in his own cadence, and is comfortable, you can then expand the movement.

Each time the rider forgets to control the cadence, it is the horse who commands.

When you are the boss of the cadence, you can do anything!

Desire to give your horse all the brilliance he is capable of.

First develop a good impulsion, this will lead to a good cadence.

The secret is to eventually do as little as possible and your horse, himself will have a good cadence for each of his paces.

With no cadence your horse will rush, he will hurry, and his paces will be stiff. But if he is in a good cadence his paces will be supple.

When one loses the cadence, and the lightness, it is because the rider has lost all his tact and is riding for the gallery, the judges, and unfortunately makes his horse a living statue.

IMPULSION

Impulsion is to have the horse in the frame you want showing every moment the same level of energy, and in the attitude you want, without the help of the aids, for the greatest length of time possible.

Impulsion is not what many people think and preach. Push the horse to take the contact and the horse becomes round, energetic and that is all?

One of the signs of impulsion is a still head.

Spectacular movement and force…the person who knows nothing says that the horse is forward.

The horse that has impulsion and engages the hind quarters will find the contact.

You lose the impulsion because you move your body more than the horse's.

And when you are the boss of the Cadence you can do anything!

When the horse develops impulsion and lightness you achieve harmony between the hindquarters and the forehand.

LIGHTNESS — COLLECTION

For myself, Lightness is defined as the horse's acceptance of the following conditions: activity of the hind legs, and suppleness of the horse's back, both of which permit him to have from the start of his training a degree of collection, without making him give by pulling him in and under, nor by the direct intervention of the rider's hand!

Lightness can only be achieved by a perfectly balanced horse. That is, a horse working in his own balance.

When the horse develops impulsion and lightness you achieve harmony between the hindquarters and the forehand. The increased engagement of the hindquarters lightens the forehand and you can ride like a king and the horse carries you like a king!

For some riders, lightness is the horse's obedience to the leg aids and the control of rider's hands, which purely direct with the feeling that they are speaking to the horse.

If a horse is light, mobile, and flexing the three joints in his hindquarters correctly, then the most difficult movements of dressage are not too difficult.

COLLECTION

Collection is not just the shortening of the horse. That is not sufficient to develop collection. The horse's back should arch/round like a cat's back.

The rider must always have in his head that to train a dressage horse is to push, to take, and to give.

To Push — by gentle action of the rider's back and seat.

To Take — the closing (flexing) of the fingers with a still hand, the result of a correctly placed arm and elbow, (near the body) the flexion of the waist, and the position of the chest, but all calm and relaxed.

To Give — when the fingers relax a little and give, the contact becomes softer, the horse maintains the increased energy and his collection does not alter.

The horse will then remain in that collection with the rider relaxed for some moments; the length of time depends on his training.

Certain horses move slower than others and, in order to have a horse truly in collection, one must work him in his own cadence.

To obtain collection, excessive force, pulling by the arm muscles of the rider will never give the horse fluidity or brilliance in his movements.

True and correct collection is only obtained when the loins, the hindquarters and the hocks become flexible. Then, the hindquarters can energetically push the horse forward as the shoulders become lightened and free.

When the two hind legs have been developed to work equally, the collection at the trot can be developed.

Cadence and suspension develop a harmonious collected trot and the rider needs only to give the minimum of light aids.

Look at the same movements with a rider who is kicking and pulling on the reins and we see tenseness, stiffness and a lack of harmony.

The relaxation of the legs and hands of the rider *(descente de main)* is the proof of real collection and that collection is the poetry of impulsion.

THE CENTRE LINE

A STRAIGHT line is a straight line is a straight line.

Horses never go straight by force.

The rider is more attentive to maintain his horse very straight on the centre line than on the wall. Because of this attention of the rider to straightness, the horse stays more attentive and receptive.

When you ride in the manège or in a rectangle you must not forget to frequently ride the centre line in all three gaits.

When you turn onto the centre line, in the middle of the short side, you must turn by your outside rein around your inside leg, so the horse takes in the beginning of the centre line a very straight line.

If the horse keeps his cadence and his lightness in a position absolutely straight, then in the course of training, the centre line can be a better place to ask the first few steps of piaffe instead of on the wall.

A horse is straight...

• when he maintains his cadence on the straight line;

• when he is no longer heavy on the hand on the straight line;

• when on a centre line he can immediately begin a six meter volte to right or to left.

This work using the Centre Line is sometimes forgotten by riders, it is very important work in the training of the horse.

Start to ask for Shoulder-In on a large circle, then on a small circle and always with the outside rein, in order to be able to put the horse back very straight on the Centre Line.

A straight line is a straight line is a straight line!

PIROUETTES

WHEN the horse is relaxed in the preceding exercises at halt and rein back you can begin to ask the half pirouette at walk.

On the long side, ask with a half halt, push take and give, and gently alternate the weight of the buttocks and also the action of the legs, with each step of the horse.

If the rider's hand is not hard and does not block the forehand, the horse will execute a half pirouette without blocking the hindquarters.

To begin walk pirouettes it is necessary to have a correct collected walk and that the collected walk is not just a slower walk.

In both the walk and canter pirouettes, the horse's outside shoulder moves around the hindquarters.

Touch one step, give another, allow the horse to step without resistance.

CANTER PIROUETTE

THE canter pirouette is without doubt one of the most difficult exercises to execute.

Rare is the horse, which executes the pirouette without the whole horse bobbing up and down.

In the true pirouette, the horse remains round and light.

For the pirouette to be done correctly, it is necessary, of course, that the preparation be progressive and done with care and attention.

The action of the inside leg is very important since it must maintain each quarter of the pirouette.

It must stop the horse from leaning with his shoulders towards the inside and must keep the impulsion.

The rider's torso is positioned slightly towards the inside. The rider must look a little sideways and back, neither up nor down excessively, and without tilting the head towards the inside shoulder. The outside leg must act without force so that the horse enters the pirouette in a relaxed canter and perfectly straight. The hindquarters must be flexed, but not sitting down or crouching.

The F.E.I. states that one must execute the pirouette in a certain canter and move forward from the pirouette in the same canter.

I agree completely with this, but most times riders arrive for the pirouette in a canter without sufficient cadence and sitting, and with aids that are too strong. They then ask for a pirouette in which the horse is crouched and with a different rhythm and mechanism of the canter. The horse then leaves the pirouette again in a different rhythm of canter.

It is because of the tendency to produce these different rhythms that I advise you to place more importance and emphasis on the shortening of the canter than in other exercises.

To enter the pirouette through light and delicate aids and during the pirouette, practice relaxing the hands (*descente de main*) in order to prevent the up and down movements of the head and neck of the horse.

If the aids of the rider are harsh, the pirouette will be incorrect.

But if the rider gives delicate and precise aids, then the horse will remain round and supple in his pirouette.

If the aids of the rider are harsh, the pirouette will be incorrect. But if the rider employs delicate and precise aids, the horse will remain round and supple in his pirouette.

Give to your horse all the brilliance he is capable of attaining.

PIAFFE

THE piaffe is one of the most brilliant airs that a horse can execute when it is high and slow.

Not all horses are capable of producing such a piaffe. However, a small piaffe, with quicker steps is within the scope of nearly all horses.

One of the greatest secrets of obtaining the first steps of piaffe easily from the horse is not to forget the formula "prepare and allow it to happen." This means that the energy and the roundness of the horse are such, that it makes the piaffe possible at the time of arriving on the spot, through leaving the horse alone, so that he remains mobile.

This formula will be very difficult for riders who do not have the permanent concern and attention for lightness. Because of this, the piaffe remains for them an enigma.

The main points in the first commands for the piaffe is to have the wisdom to stop before the horse wishes to stop. It is necessary that the horse learns to piaffe, of course with energy. But that in his mind, he remains calm and confident in his head as if he were doing simple work at walk.

It is necessary to only ask more steps or, to ask more elevation very progressively.

It is a serious error at the beginnings of the commands of the piaffe to have the childish pretension of putting the horse forward by asking the horse to go from the piaffe to a medium or extended trot.

It is by stopping him and loosening the reins, it is by leaving the piaffe at a walk on a long rein, or by a collected trot that one establishes a desire in the horse to remain in the piaffe.

To obtain piaffe, the use by the rider of a long whip or two whips must be made with tact and extreme delicacy.

Sometimes it is not a touch, just the sound or movement of the whip beside the legs or near the hindquarters, without touching the horse, which can give the result.

The greatest difficulty in obtaining the piaffe is caused by the rider's hands which are almost always, not light enough.

If the horse already knows a little piaffe in hand easily, he will piaffe easily mounted.

It is a question of the association of the riding whip with the action of your torso, your hands and your legs, and to progressively eliminate the use of the riding whip when the horse adequately understands the aids for the piaffe.

If the horse does not know the piaffe in hand, it is necessary to think carefully about how one is to ask for the first steps, so that the horse remains relaxed in his head and not tense.

If this does occur, it will cause the horse to always perform piaffe in a tense and constrained manner, with a desire to escape the exercise. This will make the resulting piaffe a badly taught trick rather than a brilliant result of collection.

I am not talking here of the case of the horse that can do piaffe naturally, the one so well balanced that a rider, with tact and perfect co-ordination is capable of asking the piaffe at any time or phase of training.

With the horse that is tense and constrained and not relaxed in his piaffe, it is best to teach the passage first.

And when this passage is well established, well cadenced and sustained, one will reduce the forward steps of passage and develop a good piaffe.

It is very important to remember that the horse should not be excited by the piaffe. This precaution must not be neglected so that his walk does not lose any of its regularity.

When beginning piaffe, never demand too much. More height, more brilliance should only be asked for after the horse has confidence to stay calm and relaxed in his mind and in his independent balance.

The piaffe should be taught as a gymnastic exercise. It will help the horse become obedient to the aids, happily accepting the requests of the rider and it will help develop the gaits of the horse in an harmonious manner.

The more brilliant the horse, the softer the aids.

PASSAGE

FOR the development of the passage it is necessary, in the beginning, for the strides to remain short, and with lowered hindquarters feeling the energy go from the lowered hindquarters up to the raised forehand, and not towards the front in a level [horizontal] balance.

Later, when the horse is confident, you can ask for a longer or shorter, lighter passage without the horse losing collection.

Unfortunately, the rider, not familiar or with little knowledge often believes that longer steps that seem more spectacular are the desired results at the beginning of the teaching of passage.

The lowering of the hind fetlock joint and the flexing of this joint can be observed. It is the proof that the horse remains with his haunches low and in the true collection in passage.

The passage must be high, but when too much height is asked, the suspension is sacrificed and that is the result of force.

You must give to each horse all the brilliance he is capable of attaining, but never exceed his limits.

The more brilliant the horse, the softer the aids.

Keep the horse straight, do not let him put weight in front.

The horse must stay calm, relaxed, straight, light, with even rhythm and suspension.

Do not use force.

Stop before the horse wishes to stop, and directly afterwards, stay at a halt with long, relaxed reins.

PILLARS

IN modern equitation we can go without Pillars, but one must never forget what the old Masters said, "pillars give spirit to the horses."

Pillars can be used as a way to help the horse in his piaffe when he has already learned it in the manège, without the pillars.

Your horse which can calmly piaffe alone without saddle or bridle in the pillars, without upsetting himself will round himself, more and more, and will develop his muscles in a "good way."

I do not agree at all, to put horses in the pillars with fixed side reins, this method has too much constraint.

The horse that can piaffe in the pillars without the restriction of fixed reins and without stepping backwards, and without pulling on the reins used to attach him to the pillars is preparing and developing his own balance and collected gaits.

When the horse begins to piaffe nearly correctly in the pillars we dispense with the extra person in front of the horse, remove the lunge that prevented the horse stepping forwards and just use the leads attaching the horse from the cavesson to the pillars.

Frequently, we ought to pat the horse and also let the horse stay at the halt for a long time without moving.

Instead of touching the horse on the chest with the whip to have the front legs raise a little more, it is more useful to give some little touches on the withers.

At the end of each lesson, make the horse walk through the pillars two or three times, remaining very calm and straight.

Reward often.

Pillars can be used as a way to help a horse in his piaffe when he has already learned it in the manège without the pillars.

SPANISH WALK

I CONSIDER the Spanish walk a very useful gymnastic exercise for any horse.

It improves the suppleness of the horse's shoulders.

However, we must remember that the horse must be calm and that the Spanish Walk, like the normal walk, has four equal, even beats.

Horses that are croup high and restricted in the stride of the forelegs will be helped by the gymnastic exercise of the Spanish Walk.

Other horses with poor collection due to bad training with the forelegs too far under the body will also be helped.

The cadence, the extension and the height are the qualities of a correct Spanish Walk.

I consider the Spanish Walk a very useful gymnastic exercise for any horse.

END OF CLASS

End of class and Nuno Oliveira gives every horse beans and a pat.

MY FRIENDS ... THANK YOU!

And, always, afterwards...

...a caress with love

NUNO OLIVEIRA
1925-1989

www.ingramcontent.com/pod-product-compliance
Lightning Source LLC
Chambersburg PA
CBHW060517300426
44112CB00017B/2701